Hot Air Ballooning

The balloon is ready for launching in the cool, still morning air.

Hot Air Ballooning

by Peter B. Mohn

Library of Congress Catalog Card Number: 75-16086
International Standard Book Number: 0-913940-30-5

Reprinted 1978

Crestwood House, Inc., Mankato, Minnesota 56001

Hot Air Ballooning

Balloons are a rare sight. When they fly, they usually draw a crowd.

Two people stood in a narrow, shallow wicker basket resting on the ground. Above them towered an immense, 50-foot-high, 45-foot wide bag full of hot air.

Right over their heads, a pair of gas burners hissed gently on top of an aluminum frame.

"Ready?" asked the pilot. Passenger and ground crew nodded yes. The pilot reached up and pulled on a red handle. The gas burners roared, disturbing the quietness of the early morning.

Slowly, the big bag above the pilot and passenger rose, taking them and the wicker basket with it. The ground crew, who would follow the balloon along country roads, steadied the basket until it rose beyond their reach.

The balloon continued to climb, and as it cleared the trees, a gentle morning breeze caught it. It began to drift slowly away. Those in the air waved at the people on the ground, and another balloon flight had begun.

Later in the day, the pilot would begin looking for a suitable landing place. Using his gas burners to produce warm air and keep the balloon up, then his vent valve to let hot air out and cause the balloon to go down, the pilot would try to put the delicate airship down "on the spot."

Hot air ballooning was invented more than 100 years ago. At first, it was thought to be a novelty. But generals in wartime found balloons were valuable in being able to tell where their enemies were located.

Hot air balloons can be decorated to suit the owner's ideas. This one has many colored pennants.

Around the United States and Europe, people would take hot air balloons to cities and fairs and make ascensions, or flights. Many of them were called "barnstormers," but the name barnstormer became more popular when daredevil aircraft pilots started appearing at the same events.

Not everyone liked hot air balloonists. Many weren't used to seeing people floating through the air. Sometimes the balloonists were treated badly and their flimsy balloons were destroyed.

As time went on, balloons were used for research. Scientists found ways of controlling the flight of balloons. These large, slow-moving airships made perfect platforms from which to study the land beneath them.

As the 20th century grew older, the hot air balloon gave way to the helium-filled research balloon. Many people rode these balloons to the limits of the atmosphere to do research on high altitudes, the sun and each other.

One man even jumped out of a balloon which was more than 100,000 feet above the earth to see what would happen to him when he did it! The man opened his parachute at quite a low altitude and lived to tell his story.

Balloons of various kinds are extremely valuable to our weather forecasters. In most cases, the balloons are small and unmanned.

Today many people are riding in hot air balloons just for the fun of it!

When ballooning around cities, the balloonists
must be careful to avoid trees and power lines.

Sport ballooning, as it is called, does not have many followers. Those who do it are very enthusiastic about the sport.

Unlike many other outdoor sports, sport ballooning is regulated by the government. Every balloon pilot must go through a regular training period to get a license. Before the license is issued, the pilot must take and pass examinations.

The examinations, if passed, show that the pilot knows how to fly a balloon and knows the laws which govern balloon flights. The pilot must also pass a physical examination.

What makes a hot air balloon fly?

Warm air rises. If we heat a lightweight bag full of air, it will rise. If we have enough hot air inside the bag, it will lift more than its own weight.

The reason a hot air balloon is so big is that it needs a large volume of hot air to lift the basket under it (sometimes called the gondola) and the people and equipment it carries.

An average size hot air balloon may be as big as 50,000 cubic feet. That would be enough air to fill a room 50 feet wide, 100 feet long and 10 feet high!

The hotter the air inside the balloon, the more it can lift. The difference in temperature of the outside air helps, too. The colder the outside air, the more the balloon can lift.

This means the best time of day for launching a balloon often will be in the early morning hours before the sun comes up and warms the outside air.

Late fall, winter and early spring are the best seasons for ballooning because the air tends to be cooler.

A hot air balloon is quite a simple thing.

There's the hot-air bag which holds everything up. Attached to it with shrouds is the basket, or gondola in which we ride.

The gondola has places to sit and some instruments. Also on board will be the fuel tanks with the gas to heat the air.

The instruments will include an altimeter, which tells us how high we are, a rate of climb or descent indicator which tells us whether we're going up or down and how fast, a compass which tells us the direction we are traveling and a pyrometer, which tells us the air temperature in the balloon.

On a frame above the gondola we'll find the gas burners and the control handles we'll use to maneuver the balloon. Much of the time, the only maneuvering we can do effectively is up or down.

Usually, the burner control and the vent control will be close together. When we want the balloon to rise, we'll pull the burner control handle, called the "blast valve."

When the blast valve is pulled, the gas burners above our heads roar into life and heat pours into the bag above. The warmer air will make us rise.

When the vent control is pulled, it opens a hole either in the top or the side of the balloon, allowing hot air to spill out. This causes us to descend.

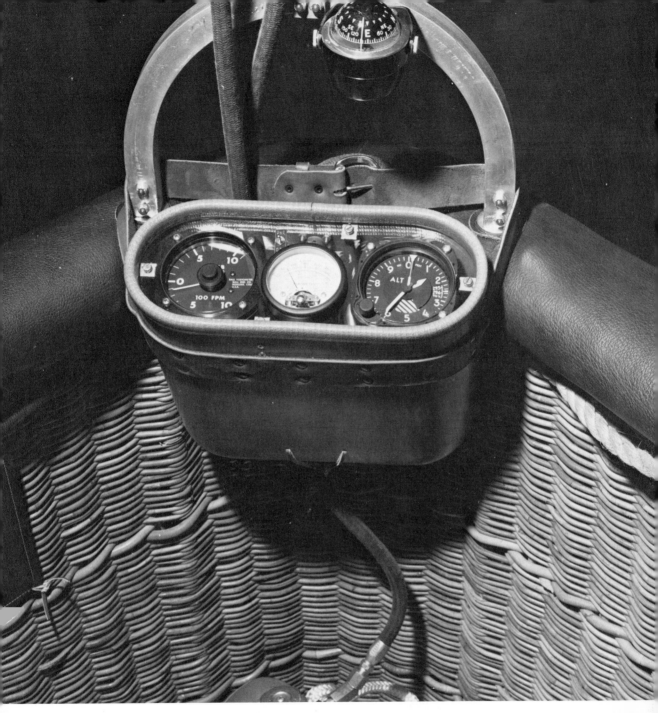

These are the instruments a balloon must
have. At the top is a compass. Below, from left
to right, are a rate of climb or descent
indicator, a pyrometer (temperature gauge) and
an altimeter, to tell how high the balloon is.

The only other control we have is called the "rip panel." Used only on landings, the rip panel control is placed away from the other two so we can't pull it by accident.

In most sport balloons, the rip panel is carefully put in place and checked just before the flight. On landing, the pilot can pull one whole piece right out of the bag to cause the balloon to deflate quickly.

When the hot air is let out of the balloon quickly, the balloon and its passengers are less likely to be dragged over the ground after they touch down. Just the same, this can happen in high winds.

An open, flat area is the best place for both takeoffs and landings. Balloonists avoid the water, except, perhaps, in emergencies.

Why go ballooning?

A balloon pilot will tell you the sport is worthwhile just for the quiet and peace that is found when you're just floating with the wind.

Balloonists are a rare breed in the world. Of all people who can fly some kind of airship, there are fewer hot air balloonists than any other kind of pilot.

A balloon doesn't cost much to fly. The liquefied propane (LP) gas burned to warm the air costs far less than regular aviation gasoline. The balloonist has to pay for no more than the operations of the ground crew which follows the flight.

Most sport balloons don't fly too high. Many times, a balloon floating along will cast a shadow on the ground that people will notice. Looking up, they see the balloon. Many people haven't seen hot air balloons outside of the movies or television so there is great interest.

Wherever the winds blow, the balloons go.

The start of a balloon race at the St. Paul,
Minn. Winter Carnival.

Balloonists also compete. They try to set records. They have meets in which they race, have spot landing contests and other events. Most of all, it's fun just getting together with other balloonists and telling stories.

What do we need to go ballooning?

We already know a balloon, gondola, burners and instruments are necessary. If ours is to be a "solo" flight (one without a licensed pilot) we have to have a license to fly a balloon.

We will need an "inflation blower." This is a gasoline engine-operated fan which is used to put cold air into the balloon while it's flat on the ground.

And we need a ground crew. After landing there's no way we can pick up the gondola and all that billowing material and carry it back to the launching site. Most ground crews use pickup trucks.

Many balloonists also carry two-way radios so they can stay in touch with their ground crews and other aircraft.

We'll need warm clothing and lifejackets, if we should happen to come down on a lake or river.

Once the inflation blower has begun to make the nylon fabric of our balloon rise off the ground and billow, we turn the burners on and begin to heat the air. As the air inside the balloon warms, it gradually begins to rise off the ground.

After that, it's up to us to decide how high we fly. Some times, the winds will blow in different directions at different heights so we can decide, somewhat, which direction to go.

Ballooning races can draw contestants from all
over the nation and the world.

What's a balloon meet like?

For one thing, it's about as colorful an event as we'll ever see. Balloon designs and colors are as different as the faces and personalities of their pilots. Most of the colors are the brightest that can be found. Many times the balloons even have names.

The balloonists and their ground crews often have their own uniforms as colorful as their balloons.

As launch time begins, the crews begin to lay out the limp nylon bags, check out the rip panels and start the inflation blowers.

Minutes later, the roars of the inflation blowers will begin to die as hot air inflation begins. Then slowly and majestically, the large, colorful balloons begin to stand up straight.

The ground crews scurry around, helping to put gear into the gondolas while the pilots climb aboard. If they're having a balloon race, all the balloons will be released at once. on a signal from the race officials.

Another kind of race is called the "hare and hounds" race. In the hare and hounds race, one balloon called the hare, is released first. The hare flies for a period of time and lands.

The hounds, after they are released, try to locate the hare and land near it. The balloonist who lands closest to the hare is the winner of the race.

The hare and hounds race is probably the most exciting of the balloon races, and calls for the most skill. The pilots have to be very accurate in their judgement of wind currents and altitudes as they follow the hare.

Once all balloons have landed and the judges have measured distances of the hounds from the hare, the winner is announced and the balloons are taken back to the starting point for the next event.

Spot landing contests are usually held in front of a crowd. The spot is designated in front of the spectator area and each pilot tries to land the balloon as close to the spot as possible. The pilot that lands the balloon closest to the spot wins the event.

Balloonists enjoy gathering at meets for friendly competition, but there's another form of trying to outdo the others. That's in record-setting.

There are world's records for the length of a hotair balloon flight, the maximum height of an ascension and the longest time spent in the air.

When a balloon pilot goes after a record, certain instruments must be in the gondola for proof. A barograph is one of the instruments. From the tracing on the barograph paper, experts can tell how high and how long the balloon has flown.

After a record flight, the pilot must submit reports from witnesses and all other information about the flight to a board of experts. The board decides if the data are correct and awards the record.

Like many records, a ballooning world's record may not mean too much to anyone but a balloonist. But it's one more way for a person to find freedom in the air and satisfaction from doing something different.

A St. Paul, Minnesota family has made a career out of ballooning.

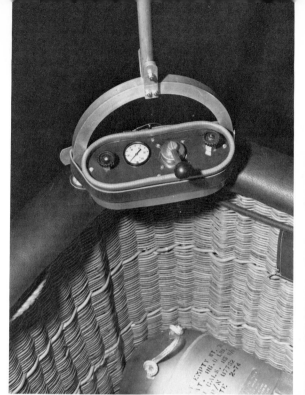

Top left, the balloon's burner control with fuel
tank valves and temperature indicator.
Right, the "rip panel" used to quickly deflate
the balloon. Bottom left, the burners.
Right, the vent.

Donna Wiederkehr, who set world ballooning
records at age 14.

Remember the movie, "Around the World in 80 Days?" This balloon was used for Captain Phileas Phogg's trip over the Alps.

Matt Wiederkehr holds 22 world records for hot air balloonists. His daughter, Donna, set two altitude records, six distance records and six duration records when she was 14 years old, in 1975.

In setting those records, Donna flew a small AX-2 balloon, with about a 14,000 cubic foot capacity to a height of 1,953 feet. Her flight lasted two hours and 40 minutes. She traveled 11.19 miles on her flight.

In 1974, Donna's sister Denise, 16, undertook a balloon flight for the benefit of a high school class-mate who had cancer.

Mat and Denise Wiederkehr, also
record-holding balloonists.

To help with medical expenses, students at Hill-Murray high school in St. Paul had pledged to raise $105 for every hour Denise stayed in the air.

So on March 23, 1974, Denise Wiederkehr took off. She flew for 11 hours, 10 minutes. When she landed her balloon, she was 228.04 miles from her take-off point. Later, it was determined she had set six distance records and six duration records for the AX-6 balloon. The distance record was previously held by her father.

What was more important to Denise and her fellow students is that she had helped to raise more than $1,500 for a classmate.

Less than two weeks before Denise's flight, her father smashed a series of records by flying another balloon for 16 hours and 16 minutes. He broke the old record by more than five hours! He traveled a distance of 337.23 miles on the flight.

Matt Wiederkehr travels around the country much of the year and gives ballooning demonstrations.

There are still some unconquered frontiers in ballooning. No one has crossed the Atlantic Ocean in a balloon of any kind, but several persons died trying.

People have tried to fly balloons across many different areas. The English Channel between England and France has been crossed by balloons many times.

Even the Atlantic has been crossed by lighter-

Inflating the balloon. The person at right is
operating a blower. Once partially inflated by
the blower, the balloonists will begin to heat
the air inside the balloon to give it lift.

than-air-craft, but these were powered with engines.
They were called dirigibles. One of the most famous
was the Hindenburg, a German dirigible (or blimp)
which crashed in flames in New Jersey.

One of the biggest reasons for the Hindenburg
disaster was that the balloon was filled with hydrogen,
a gas that burns very viciously. A number of people
were killed in the crash.

Dirigibles were used for anti-submarine patrol during World War II, but they were much safer than the Hindenburg. The few dirigibles still in the air, like the Goodyear blimp, use helium gas which doesn't burn at all.

And in recent years, some manufacturers have developed hot air blimps with engines. These blimps are used mostly for exhibitions and displays.

Not all balloons have to fly outdoors. Here, Denise Wiederkehr is getting ready to make a solo flight inside the Houston, Texas Astrodome!

This balloon carries the old-fashioned wicker basket-type gondola.

Even though a hot air balloon may sound more like something out of the past, it is not. Both hot air balloons and gas-filled balloons are used for carrying loads in and out of places that can't be reached on the ground.

These balloons are usually "tethered," or attached to the ground with heavy ropes on immense reels. Once they rise above the obstacles on the ground, they are pulled from one location to the next by the ropes.

Using a balloon for such a purpose is much less expensive than using a helicopter.

Because balloons move slowly and drift with the wind, they are sometimes mistaken for unidentified flying objects. More often than not, these are gas-filled research balloons made of shiny plastic. Some research balloons stand taller than some high-rise buildings.

As the air warms inside an inflating balloon, it
begins to rise higher, until it stands
straight up.

These tall gas balloons are usually launched from
deep pits or canyons in the early morning hours.
That way, the crews who launch them don't have to
worry about wind currents thrashing the fragile plastic balloon.

It may happen that some day, you will see a colorful balloon floating gently overhead. Or at a fair
or an air show you might even have a chance to take
a brief ride in one.

Once you get your feet off the ground, you may
never want to return!

The balloon drifts freely across the sky at sunrise. It's pretty to see. But what if we were up there?